THE RIVER HILLS
AND BEYOND

The River Hills and Beyond

Lou V P Crabtree
1-13-99

Poems

Love and Peace

Lou V. Crabtree

Sow's Ear Press
Abingdon / Virginia / 1998

Acknowledgments

Thanks to the editors of the following periodicals, in which some of the poems in this volume first appeared: *Appalachian Journal, Laurel Review, New Virginia Review, Now & Then, Shenandoah,* and *Sow's Ear Poetry Review.* "Salvation" appeared in *Appalachia Inside Out: A Sequel to Voices From the Hills, Vol. 2, Culture and Custom,* Ed. Robert J. Higgs, Ambrose N. Manning, and Jim Wayne Miller, Knoxville, University of Tennessee Press, 1995.

DRAWINGS BY NANCY GARRETSON

Publisher's Cataloging-in-Publication
(Provided by Quality Books, Inc.)

Crabtree, Lou V.
    The river hills and beyond : poems / Lou Crabtree -- 1st ed
    p. cm.
    ISBN: 1-885912-19-6

1. Appalachian Mountains--Poetry.   I. Title

PS3553.R19R58.1998   811'.54
                                        QB198-1400

First Edition

THE RIVER HILLS AND BEYOND Copyright © Lou V. Crabtree, 1998
All rights reserved. No part of this book may be reproduced in any manner whatsoever without the permission of the publisher, except in the case of quotations in critical articles or reviews. Information may be obtained from The Sow's Ear Press, 19535 Pleasant View Dr., Abingdon, Virginia 24211-6827. The Sow's Ear Press is a component of The Word Process, a non-profit Virginia corporation. Manufactured in the USA.

for—
LEE SMITH
DAN LEIDIG
BEN JENNINGS
LAWRENCE REYNOLDS
and all writers using and loving words

and special thanks to—
Chris Brown, Betty Davison, Judy Miller,
Cleo Partington, and Barbara Smith

PUBLISHERS' PREFACE

When poet Dan Leidig suggested to us, after a 1997 celebration honoring Lou Crabtree, that the power and variety and fascination of her poems cried out for a book, we knew immediately that he was right, and that we should publish it. The project which began then has been a community effort from the beginning.

The book is made possible by generous contributions from Leidig, Lee Smith, Nell Maiden, Harriette Horner, Joan Horsch, and Mary Ann Artrip. Shirley Abell has over the years turned many of the manuscripts into typescripts. For this project Nell Maiden helped also with the next step, turning typescripts into computerscripts. Nancy Garretson created and contributed the cover and section title drawings. And the Foreword and Introduction express from two different points of view something of what Lou Crabtree has meant in the literary and spiritual life of this small town on this medium-sized planet in this mysterious cosmos, as she weaves the words that link our inner spaces to outer spaces, that link our stories to The Story.

In editing we have tried to honor the poet's decisions and to follow her advice to "make it easy for the reader." We regret only that the book represents a relatively small selection from a rich body of work created over a lifetime of vision and revision. Finally, if there are errors, they are ours.

Ann & Larry Richman
ABINGDON, VIRGINIA

Contents

Foreword by Dan Leidig   i

Introduction by Lee Smith   vii

I. The River Hills

Smith Creek No. 1	3
Smith Creek No. 2	5
Now I Lay Me Down to Sleep	7
Husband	8
April Dawn Clifton	9
Kudzu	10
All the Little Birdies and Beasties	11
Son	12
Love	13
Love No. 3	14
Love No. 4	15
Asking a Daisy	16
He Cut My Garden Down	17
Sister	19
Mosquito on Nose	20
Playmates	21
Soapstone Hollow	22
Devil's Den Hollow	23
Hant Hollow	25
Salvation	26
Sports Widow	27
I Am Seeing Me	28
Last Party	29

II. And Beyond

Refugees	33
Noah's Animals	34
Boy	37
Shulammite Girl	38
Indian—Ulagu	39
Soldier Soldier No. 2	40
Soldier Soldier No. 3	42
No. 10 Boom Boom Girl	43
Nit of a Louse	45
Learning	46
Mutations	48
from Pluto	49
from Lost in Space	50
from Riding in Space	51
from Circles	52
Notes	53

Foreword

Just as Lou Crabtree's book of stories, *Sweet Hollow*, tempers sweetness with the pulse of a darkened vale, the title of this collection of poems, *The River Hills and Beyond*, hints at paradox: beyond the salubrious hills where we celebrate the joys of the human pilgrimage lies the valley of the shadow. For this seasoned poet the connection is continuous. The simple, indivisible beauty of a "bubby bush" at her doorstep recalls a "life-long romance / [that] is always in my mind." It is a mind that also reminds us, as in "Mutations," that we are capable of cutting "the earth loose from its hinges," of producing a progeny of blind old men who "play / with rats that have no hair or eyes." Within the vast range from romantic exuberance to tragic flaw to adventures in the realms of space, the poet's deft hand, guided by the wisdom of experience, explores with wit, candor, and pathos the ageless arenas of childhood, love, belief, nature, tragedy, and death.

The poems in Part 1, "The River Hills," derive from the lore and life of those hills with that certain, back-of-the-hand authority that comes from a native highlander who has spent time "tracking the turkey hen / over ridges," "seen a locust hill by moonlight," watched the bluebird come "from nowhere to / Put his whistle in the mockingbird's throat," and who has chronicled with awe an unnoticed world where "A moth settles in the thistle briars." These poems are the bounty of

>... years of planting harvesting
>Breathing touching among our meanderings
>In and out of lives where we pursued
>All strange and wonderful things
>Down deep into the mysterious dark
>Where the roots wind about the heart.

It is indeed, in the words of William Stafford, the "heart's own true country" to which Lou Crabtree has invited us.

In our "meanderings in and out of lives" we discover delightful episodes of sibling rivalries, as in "Now I Lay Me Down to Sleep." There is a lovely childlike prayer that invokes the Lord "who rides the crest of the storm" .... to "Collect ... / In the great apron of your lap / All the little birdies and beauties." There is grisly fun in a child's clandestine visit to the devil's den just "to show he wasn't scared." And there are engagements with grotesqueries involving "a clubfoot dwarf" who had "growed a horn" and who, "They said, ... ate rattlesnakes." But more foreboding than the "hant hollows" of childhood imagination is the shadow that enfolds April Dawn whose

>...eyes never opened
>on this world you are leaving
>Some blemish in the genes
>   in your grandmother, I have heard,
>   .... this curse
>In the twin you left behind.

And more chilling still is the stark psychodrama compressed into the few taut lines of "Playmates," in which the protagonist is drawn to view the body of "so rude a man" . . . [who] "in his casket . . . / lay with one finger missing; that part / I felt a kinship with, of sorts, / like that finger was lost in me . . . . making me, after sixty years, / go to look."

The depths and shoals in the river of love and marriage generate some of the book's most powerful poems. There is "Always and forever love / playing in my mind / like the blue lizard family / frolicking . . . ." Elsewhere, the warm sun drenches a red salamander just "as my lover drenches me with delight." And there is a lovely country epithalamium in which

> Old Nan had slick ironed
>   my white blouse
> The wind laved my blue skirt
>   around my legs
> as the sun   smiled a laddie
>   coming up the path
>   with a new hat on.

Yet the frequent outcome of such romance is oppression: "I hated those years of no new dresses / . . . the years of borning . . . by myself with no doctor / . . . . Doing everyday the same thing the same way / the milking morning and night / Sunday too" for a lifetime: "Now I wonder why no one / Ever said to me   you are young." There is wistfulness and latent sensuality in "Husband," where a widow reflects on how "eyes, taboos, codes" prevented her from ever seeing her husband naked until "I saw his yellow back / . . . when the liver cancer / had him. / Not even in dreams / does he ever come / Gloriously in naked good health." In one of the collection's most powerful poems an embittered, angry woman, impoverished at the hands of an evil man, is forced to send her seven-year-old daughter to seek refuge at "a house in the far valley / 'Go there, / Go to that house. Try to stay the winter.'" She cannot forgive, even in the aftermath of the man's violent death. "Old granny honed me / 'Don't let his rage into you.' / I said / *He did not have to cut / my garden down.*"

The moving final poem in "The River Hills" is vintage Crabtree in its no-nonsense directness and its discriminating simplicity. One's funeral, the "Last Party," should be "Just a little get-together . . . . Just some old women friends / to come and bide a spell . . . . When news and gossip peters out / I would like sitting a last hour with me / Some old women I have known."

The second section, "And Beyond," is a remarkable ingathering of poems from across a universe of time and place, emboldened by a singular wit and imagination. Old Noah, "his galluses hitched high," dodges the stampede of animals while Mrs. Noah wonders, "Who is going to clean up this mess?" From a cluster of forthright poems on the tragedy of war an orphaned Vietnamese boy cries out for his American father: "Papa-san. . . / Each day / I bow before your picture / many times / I keep safe in box off your coat / two buttons." From another war two opposing soldiers lie dying on a battlefield that takes no notice of their profound perception: "We were poor boys / Sent to kill poor boys. / Your answer grows a weaker 'Ja.'" One of the most poignant protests in these war poems comes from a Saigon prostitute:

> When the beast, who already has the body, asks
> For the soul, I will pretend to be not sane and say,
> "I sent it already by the long-tailed blackbird, now
> Sitting on the black bough of
>   the plum tree."

Appropriately, this collection concludes with a sampling of Crabtree's recent immersion in the mythos of outer space. She begins her portrait of Pluto with a twinkle: "Not the dog. The planet." In an imaginary earth orbit the poet's whimsy warms the out-sized journey: village farms creep up the sides of Vesuvius, the aurora becomes a parking light, and the wakes of ships spread for hundreds of miles: "I see Lake Baikal / three miles deep / with 400 rivers feeding, / pushed out where continents still collide." The ultimate legacy of space may be its omnipresence as a "monument to loneliness." Only when it replicates the emblematic circles of the human adventure does space take on "perfection / connecting no end no beginning / our circular destiny."

Lou Crabtree is alternately shy, sassy, playful, profound, and spiritual. Lee Smith aptly calls her "a commotion." She is that, as these wide-ranging poems attest, and she is confirmation that in the midst of all our clamor, the voice of the authentic poet is compelling and indispensable

Dan Leidig
EMORY, VIRGINIA

Introduction

I will never forget the first time I met Lou Crabtree—a meeting which would forever change the way I thought about writing. It was the hot, muggy summer of 1980; I was in Abingdon, Virginia, for a week to teach the creative writing class which always preceded "literary day" at the Virginia Highlands Festival. I got hotter and hotter with each step up the long staircase to the room where the class would meet, above the sanctuary in the old United Methodist Church right on Main Street. Finally I made it, and surveyed the group around a big oak table. It was about what you'd expect—eight or ten people, mostly high school English teachers, some librarians, some retirees. We had already gone around the table and introduced ourselves when here came this old woman in a man's hat and bedroom shoes, grey head shaking a little with palsy, huffing and puffing, dropping notebooks and pencils all over the place, greeting everybody with a smile and a joke. She was a real commotion all by herself.

"Hello there, young lady," she said to me. "My name is Lou Crabtree, and I just love to write!" My heart sank like a stone. This is every creative writing teacher's nightmare: the nutty old lady who will invariably write sentimental drivel and monopolize the class as well.

"Pleased to meet you," I lied. The week stretched out before me, hot and intolerable, an eternity. But I had to pull myself together. Looking around at all those sweaty, expectant faces, I began, "Okay, now I know you've brought a story with you to read to the group, so let's start out by thinking about *beginnings*, about how we begin a story. . . .let's go around the room, and I want you to read the first line of your story aloud."

So we began. Nice lines, nice people. A bee hummed at the open window; a square of golden sunlight fell on the old oak table; somebody somewhere was mowing grass. We got to Lou, who cleared her throat and read this line: "Old Rellar had thirteen miscarriages and she named all of them."

I sat up. "Would you read that line again?" I asked.

"Old Rellar had thirteen miscarriages and she named all of them," Lou read.

I took a deep breath. The hair on my arms stood straight up. "Keep going," I said.

"Only of late, she got mixed up and missed some. This bothered her. She looked toward the iron bed. It had always been exactly the same. First, came the prayer, then the act with Old Man gratifying himself. . ."

She read the whole thing. It ended with the lines: "You live all your life and work things up to come to nothing. The bull calf bawled somewhere."

I had never heard anything like it.

"Lou," I asked her after class, "have you written anything else? I'd like to see it."

The next day, she brought a suitcase. And there it all was, poems and stories written on every conceivable kind of notebook and paper, even old posters and shirtbacks.

Lou grinned at me. "This ain't all, either," she said. The next day, she brought more.

All that week, I read these poems and stories, immersing myself in Lou's primal, magic world of river hills and deep forest, of men and women and children as elemental as nature itself, of talking animals and ghosts, witchcraft and holiness. For Lou Crabtree was that rarity—a writer of perfect pitch and singular knowledge, a real artist. And most amazing of all (to me, anyway, simultaneously reading the proofs of a mediocre novel of my own) she had written all this with no thought of publication. Writing is how she lives, it's what she lives by.

"I just write for my own enjoyment," Lou told me that first time I interviewed her nearly twenty years ago. "It gives me pleasure in my soul. I think the best writing time is in the night time. And it is a wonderful time between twelve o'clock and maybe four... It is a very strange feeling when all the world is asleep but you. You feel like you're in touch with something special. And then as I write, I don't know what time it is, what day it is. It is that thing of getting out of yourself, of getting out of the world, going out of the world. You feel good, real good. You have none of these problems or hurts or anything. It is something I wish everybody could discover in their work. If they really are doing the thing they like to do, they are able to get out of their self. And it is wonderful. Very wonderful."

I asked her then what she'd do if somebody came along and told her that she couldn't write any more, "Well, you know, I would just have to *sneak!*" she said.

For the first time, I understood the therapeutic power of language, the importance of the writing process itself. Later, I would write a novel named *Fair and Tender Ladies* in which my main character writes letters in order to make sense of her life, in much the same way Lou has always written her poems and stories.

The passage of time adds a special poignancy to Lou's work. In "Smith Creek No. 1," for instance, she tells how she "loathed" life on the farm at Smith Creek, "those years of borning five young ones by myself with no doctor and washing for five on a board until four o'clock, until the sun dropped behind Gumm's Hill." Hard times. Yet after the passage of many years, this period takes on a beautiful elegiac glow. "In "Smith Creek No. 2 (feeling bad about writing Smith Creek No. 1)" she is "calling back those years of planting harvesting/ Breathing touching among our meanderings/ In and out of lives where we pursued/ All strange and wonderful things/ Down deep into the mysterious dark/ Where the roots wind about the heart." The final image is one of peaceful beauty, life come gloriously full circle at last: "In Smith Creek, a scarlet leaf floats round and round."

"You know how the mist comes up and covers the land, lots of times?" Lou asked me. "Some of these people that I write about are from a long time ago, they're *not* anymore, they're just kind of like the mist that covers my mountains. Sometimes I think they may still be there in those mountains. My people may still be right there."

Lou was born on the North Fork of the Holston River, one of ten children in the Price family. "We ran all over the hills and watched from behind trees and played Indians, and I knew more flowers and animals than I did people." She went to the Radford Normal School at 16, graduating *cum laude* in three years, then returned home to teach. She also studied drama in New York for several summers. Lou married Homer Crabtree in 1942 and moved to the Smith Creek area, near where she was born. She had five children in seven years, taking a ten-year leave from teaching to "raise cattle, tobacco, and younguns." Lou has characterized her husband as a "very soft-spoken man. . . a very calm and kind man. . . a man that people would come and sit down and talk to." Later, she returned to the classroom, teaching just about every subject at every level, from a one-room school to elementary and high schools.

Lou bought her present home at 313 Valley Street for $4000, money she'd "saved up" from teaching, and moved into town in 1960 as a widow with five teenagers. Two of her children still live in the Abingdon area: George Crabtree, "who raises those old Charolais cattle"; and Jerry Crabtree, "who runs the skills center." Daughter Bonnie Sitz, a choral teacher and director, is not far away in Blacksburg. Son Hugh Crabtree, now retired from the Air Force, lives in Florida and works as a helicopter pilot for an oil company. Lou's daughter Sarah Taylor died in Richmond several years ago.

In reminiscing about the "early widow phase," Lou winks at me: "Oh, you have lots of opportunities as a young widow. They say, 'When you're old, I'll take care of you'... like hell they will! I was through and done with all that." Even after her official retirement, Lou continued to teach all manner of classes, especially enjoying the GED and English as a Second Language groups, "getting to know some gorgeous people, from Viet Nam, and Japan, and Venezuela...well, everyplace!" She was also the leader of the "Rock of Ages Band" of senior citizens, which performed all over the area.

And always, Lou was writing, her life a testament to the sustaining and revitalizing power of language. For several summers, she participated in Lawrence Reynolds' summer workshop. Her poems and essays have been widely published; LSU Press brought out her collection of stories, *Sweet Hollow*, in 1984. She has won the Virginia Cultural Laureate in Literature Award, the Governor's Award for Arts in Virginia, as well as a special award from the Virginia Highlands Festival. "Calling On Lou," a one-woman stage play celebrating her life and work, premiered at the Barter Theater and then toured Virginia; she appeared on the Today Show several years ago.

But none of this means much to Lou. She calls the current phase of her life "the porch years" and what she likes to do is what we're doing right now, sitting out on this porch where I have visited her so many summers amid the jumble of old furniture and plants and knickknacks, just talking and reading and watching the traffic pass by on Valley Street. Sometimes we sing a little. We laugh a lot. In winter, we sit inside by the heater near her sturdy bed, books and manuscripts piled everyplace. Lou has a steady stream of visitors, pilgrims like myself.

"Why, there've been people here from the Arctic regions, just dying to talk. A man was in here the other day that had climbed Mt. Everest, and a woman came who was going on the trans-Siberian railroad. I've always wanted to go on that myself," Lou tells me.

"Why not?" I ask. "A lot of people take up traveling when they retire."

"Why, I don't *have* to!" she laughs. "I have traveled all over the world right here on this porch. People talk to me, they take me to all these places that they've been to. We are in a changing time, but people do like to talk. They will come and sit down here and talk—especially if they can laugh!"

"These porch years are very creative for me," Lou continues. She also calls them her "spiritual years." Recently she has become "interested in space," even taking a course from the University of Virginia. She has written more than fifty "space poems."

When I ask why she has gotten so fascinated with space, Lou answers, "Because it's *out there*! Our universe is like a great big clock, run by God's laws of chemistry, math, biology, and science. . . now you know *He* doesn't do things mish-mash! And there'll come a day when the spirit will take leave of this old body. It's going to rise up to Paradise, and I wanted to know where Paradise was! So I've found out by science how it's going to happen. When you go faster than the speed of light, then you get younger and younger. Science and scripture agree! You're going to live forever in Paradise, and you'll be young. I can't wait!"

Lou's new interest seems to be an expansion—not a contradiction—of traditional religion. "I went to churches all my life," she tells me, mentioning the Old Centenary Methodist Church in particular. "I never went to church in my life that I wasn't helped." And now, she says, "I'm open! I'm open to everything!"

I tell Lou that I believe I finally understand something she told me so long ago: "It is a lonely road even though you have sons and daughters that you love better than your own life—that you'd give your own life for. One day you have to let them go, you let them all go." Now I'm past fifty, I know what she meant.

"Do you ever have times you can't sleep?" she asks me. "You probably don't, but you will. Well, things will rise out of the night, someway or other. All our people back of us can rise and come out in the night time awful good, and talk to us, and comfort us. Why I saw your mother one time, Lee, sitting in a rocking chair on the porch of the Martha Washington! I saw your pa driving that fancy car right up to heaven.

"We are all going in a circle," Lou believes, "and death is not the end of our circle. It is just a word that some people have. Why, it should be thought of as a beautiful part of life. I'm not a bit afraid of dying. I want to die right here in this old bed." But not anytime soon—she'd "like to make it to 2000. I'd like to see what they do and say about it!"

And meanwhile, she'll be writing.

Lee Smith
HILLSBOROUGH, NORTH CAROLINA

I. The River Hills

SMITH CREEK NO. 1

I loathed the likes of Smith Creek
        where I followed my husband to—
those years   I looked down my nose
        and revolted and seethed   until I was
        widowed   my husband taken.
I hated those years of no new dresses
        ten of them I counted
the years of borning five young ones
        by myself with no doctor.
And washing for five on a board until four o'clock
Until the sun dropped behind Gumm's Hill.
The years of tracking the turkey hen
        over ridges   finding her eggs to hatch seventy-five
to feed seventy-five   and to sell seventy-five
To go on a truck to make   seventy-five fat dinners
        for some New York Jews   at no profit to me.
Doing everyday the same thing the same way
the milking   morning and night
        Sunday too.
The thistles grew overnight—
I was the foreigner wanting to remain a foreigner
Though people returned from as far away as Missouri.
They would stand and look at the hills.
What are they looking for, I wondered,
Asking where was Pa buried?
Poking in old buildings
Grabbing at pictures I brought out
Drinking from the spring
Asking on and on questions like
        who did Uncle Jerry marry?
        how old was Cousin Jake when he died
        and what did he die of?
I could never see any proper mates for my young
        from those old maids and dirt farmers asking
        is it going to rain or not going to rain

       repeating the same tales until
I bought the piano and changed the tales
       for a while.
Now I wonder why no one
Ever said to me   you are young.
Not one ever said   you have a lot to learn.
The only thing I can say is—
I stuck.

SMITH CREEK NO. 2

(feeling bad about writing "Smith Creek No. 1")

      Calling back
Those years of planting harvesting
Breathing touching among our meanderings
In and out of lives where we pursued
All strange and wonderful things
Down deep into the mysterious dark
Where the roots wind about the heart.
Have you seen a locust hill by moonlight?
Or, the morning after it rained,
A field of purple phlox?
To think a flicker came as he did that year
And from all the fallen trees and cliffs
He chose my apple tree to live.
The bluebird came from nowhere to
Put his whistle in the mockingbird's throat.
Cardinals played red tag.
A crane came down from the mountain pass
And on one leg seemed to sleep
Eyeing fishes in the creek.
Jonquils grew beside an old house
Where women came out with baskets on their arms
Gathering cresses and shonney.

I laugh to see Bud drive the cows across the creek,
Lifting their tails to let go.
A bee is hanging to a catkin. Nearby
A red salamander from his frozen sleep
Creeps around his winter bed of rock,
the warm sun drenching him
As my lover drenches me with delight.
The seasons change and go.
The fire-eyes of an opossum glow.
In the pawpaw patch an opossum

Hangs by his tail to the limb, playing dead.
He is not dead.
Now he is hanging to my finger.
Mists rise, lift into fogs,
Lie caught in the mountain as
The crane flies up and down,
Following his black shadow.
A moth settles in the thistle briars,
In Smith Creek, a scarlet leaf floats round and round.

Now I Lay Me Down to Sleep

I'll get you

I'll get even

> *I pray the Lord*

Your time will come

Don't worry

> *My soul to keep*

You can't make me say one word

Not in our prayer

> *If I should die before I wake*

My knees are getting tired, Mother.

Bud is trying to push me over

> *I pray the Lord my soul to take*

Just watch my smoke

> *Amen*

Ps-ss-st, Bud, where are you?

HUSBAND

I never saw my husband
        naked
For all his years we were
        under eyes, taboos, codes
        Just that one time
I saw his yellow back
        as I helped him
        with his bath
when the liver cancer
        had him.
Not even in dreams
        does he ever come
Gloriously in naked good health.

APRIL DAWN CLIFTON

    (3 Years)

The significance is mine
    that April is your name
    and birthmonth
And that I chance by
    the April you died
And see the young father
    bend over you.

    You shock me lying there.

No mortician would have dared
    on a child of three.
Those must be your dark lashes
    curling upward.

    Those firm cheeks
    and that mouth
I think you should speak
    should look up and smile.

But your eyes never opened
    on this world you are leaving
Some blemish in the genes
    in your grandmother, I have heard,
And in some aunts and female cousins.
You never saw, this curse
In the twin you leave behind.

The significance is yours not mine
    April Dawn Clifton
    in the promise of your name
You should not have to wait long.

Kudzu

for Chris Brown

  They found me dead
sitting upright in my chair.
A cocoon, wound in kudzu vines.

The kudzu made a mound
of my house and car
so they did not find me
for a while.

  They looked at the vines
pushing through the window
through the cracks
  of the floor,
  under beds,
  up walls,
following, following,
wrapping, wrapping,
  choking.

  They asked questions.
Did the kudzu do this,
  strangle,
  choke her to death,
wind her in this cocoon?

  They made excuses.
She died first, perhaps,
  sitting in her chair.

What they could never know
  was how the kudzu
fit my life.

All the Little Birdies and Beasties

for Cleo Partington

Lord, who rides the crest of the storm

For those who cannot last it out
For those who cannot survive the blast

    Gather them in your lap
All the little birdies and beasties.

The trumpet blast arrives
Then passes on leaving the cold

There is no refuge under roof or rafter
Where the icicle fingers of cold
    Have not poked

The field mouse's eyes look out
    Of his nest through straw and ice
The old cock's crow freezes to a chortle
Old Jane doesn't shake out any crumbs.

Collect them, Lord,
In the great apron of your lap

All the little birdies and beasties.

Son

I was afraid
> that when it rained
> you would not be content
> to let it rain

I was fearful
> that the land too would reject you
> with floods and hail and bad seed

When overnight
> a bud appeared
> and by nightfall
> a worm had eaten
> the green of the bud
> to green his body
> I feared

I was afraid
> the land you tore from its roots
> the land you bent your strength to
> and washed out in your sweat
> could not ease the eating eating you
> could not gentle you to acceptance
> and your hurt ease into a quiet time

I was so afraid
> there would be no time ever
> when I quit filling up
> my grave with tears.

LOVE

*for Molly Sitz, June 7, 1992,
upon her marriage to Scott Moore*

They knew the answer
      before I heard the question
in the valley   in the village
      below

With church bells
      mimicking my *yes yes yes*
Old rooster tipped the top
      of the rail fence
and would not shut up
      while little chicks
turned crazy circles in the dust

Old Nan had slick ironed
      my white blouse
The wind laved my blue skirt
      around my legs
as the sun   smiled a laddie
      coming up the path
      with a new hat on.

LOVE NO. 3

What does love have
      to do with it?

A life-long romance
      is always in my mind
In the softness
      in the mouse's ear
in the bubby bush
      beside my kitchen door
in the kisses and murmurs
      and whispers among leaves

LOVE NO. 4

Always and forever love
        playing in my mind
like the blue lizard family
        frolicking delighting me
        flicking and clicking
        over the log
like the wild rose
        that bloomed only
        after night.

Asking a Daisy

       1. I love
       2. I love
       3. I love, I say
You say, you want to fall in love
You are ready, you say
       4. I love with all my heart
       5. I cast away
How will you know him
Where is he
       6. He loves
       7. She loves
       8. They both love
You want to fall in love
If you say it enough, you will
I say FALL IN LOVE
       9. They court
      10. They tarry
He loves me
He loves me not
       9. They court
      10. They tarry
      11. They quarrel
      12. They marry
Don't worry, I say
You are in love already
       He loves me
       He loves me not
       He loves me
       He loves me
       He loves me
       I am leaving out ALL the *nots*.

HE CUT MY GARDEN DOWN

    making it so
this winter was hard
so hard I sent the girl
borrowing a bit of lard
to make the water gravy

    making it so
the boy hung to me
    past his years
my blue drop of milk
    barely passing
the blue of his lips
until his skin glistened
and his leg shanks lengthened
and I wrapped him and held him
through the day as we
took on the snow's whiteness.

I walked the girl
    seven years is young
to be put with strangers
her dangers clamped on me
I walked her on the high ridge
until I saw a house in the far valley
    "Go there,
Go to that house. Try to stay the winter."
I watched her go in the snow
until she was a dot through the gate.

He did not have
    to cut my garden down
It was not the women in town
    or the liquor
or my crocheted doily he snatched
    off the mantle
        and burned in the stove

It was not the cold stove
        he stood around
        and kicked the cold stove
        cold from no wood
until the dog slunk away
        from older kicks.

They said—
        The black mare reared and
        dragged him
        as he raced up Main Street in town
        Some men brought him in
        and prepared him
        and asked did I want to look
        I did not want to see who it was
        cut my garden down.

They said—
        I must look and helped me in
        and pulled back the sheet
        so I could see where the black mare kicked
        with his black hair crushed
        and wet in the bruises
        in a pale face where all
        the rage seemed gone.

Old granny honed me
        "Don't let his rage into you."
I said
        He did not have to cut
        my garden down.

In nightmares someone comes at me
        Awake I am glad
        someone is dead
They did not have to cut my garden down.

SISTER

It was not that I minded
                being old
I just never thought of her
                that way
She came and found my bed
                to talk
She said of old sad things
And scars left on us all
My arm found the curve
                of her
And we were young again
In a cold bed on a cold night
My cold feet moved away
                from hers
It was not I minding
                being old
That I shivered as my
                little sister slept
And in the dark she did not know
                I wept.

Mosquito on Nose

Laid out in my casket.
That old mosquito
bit on my nose.
You son of a bee
You will get no blood here
for your blood bank.

Playmates

Sixty years is long to keep a memory.

In his casket, surrounded by wife and seed
                grown tall,
so rude a man, with hands of a carpenter,
lay with one finger missing; that part
I felt a kinship with, of sorts,
like that finger was lost in me.

I had run white legged
      and I was a good runner
      I later learned other ways
      to parry and pass and be coy.
      My legs carried me in wild fear
      from whatever to be fearful of.

When as playmates
      male and female, innocent both,
      he pressed his hardness upon me,
      making me, after sixty years,
      go to look.

Soapstone Hollow

(from the series, Show Me a Hollow, #3)

Go
      when leaves are down
and the grass is dead
      or you won't find it.
At the soapstone pit,
up,
      up Soapstone Hollow at dawn,
Indians come silent
      on padded feet,
and fashion pipes and bowls

There is no sound of chipping.
      If a squirrel drops a nut,
or a deer talks to her fawn
      up in the woods,
the ancient ones rise silent
and
      go.

DEVIL'S DEN HOLLOW

(from the series, Show Me a Hollow, #9)

Bud said he had been.
      I knew he hadn't.
Mama didn't allow us.
"Do not go. In bare feet,
      you will step on something.
The devil's den is up that hollow."

Bud jumped on a devil's dust bag
      to show he wasn't scared.
The spores from the devil's dust bag
      bloomed black as gunpowder.

A devil's darning needle
      visited thistles and ironweed.
Snake doctors skimmed the creek
      where sumac and poison ivy
      showed red eyes of the devil.

      Old Boss our bitch hound
got copperhead bit up Devil's Den Hollow.
      She crawled under the corncrib
      so swelled up she died.

Hunters got lost and told Bud tales
      about a clubfoot dwarf.
They said if he wasn't the devil already,
he was fast turning, with his one club foot.
They said he had a snake pit
      and ate rattlesnakes,
and was bitten so many times he didn't hurt.

I didn't go up Devil's Den Hollow
      until I was *growed*.

By then I knew a man had turned
        his pet snakes loose up there
and they had mixed and multiplied
        and bred with other snakes
        so many
farmers never let cows in to graze
        and step on and kill off the snakes.
I learned, too,
        Mama wasn't afraid of the devil.
        Just danger to bare feet.

I wrote Bud: I know you never went.
All the snakes of the world
        are in Devil's Den Hollow.
Greens, yellows, spotteds, blacks,
        working in piles,
        their coils twisting,
So you don't know if you are snake bit
        or a sting weed
or a stickle briar has snagged you.

The pupils in the snakes' eyes
        stand straight up
        finding heat and striking out.
They got cameras in their brains
        and take pictures of you.
They lie on branches of trees;
        they sun themselves on rocks;
they entwine around huckleberry bushes;
        they slither over rocks;
even goats stand on top of cliffs.

The clubfooted dwarf peeps
        from behind every tree
        in Devil's Den Hollow.
Out of his forehead, tales go,
        he has *growed* a horn.
Hurry home, Bud. I'll take you.

HANT HOLLOW

for Grace
(from the series, Show Me a Hollow, #4)

    Up Hant Hollow
where lovers go for kicks
    a full moon shines
through creaking boards of a bridge.

    Something bad
bound to happen. I know.
    Old woman killed a snake
and spoke my name
    up Hant Hollow.

    My lover called me,
called me by my name.
I better not go. I went.

I went where moon mists meander,
    creeping through boards
    of a creaking bridge,
draping trees in shrouds.

    I'm wishing
for decaying leaves to cover me,
to cover a grave and hide me,
    as bats squeak my name,
disturbing lovers
    who go for kicks.
Who go for kicks up Hant Hollow.

SALVATION

for Lawrence Reynolds

Jesus Jesus Jesus   I got something
        this old body   aint so important
in this old body   I feel holiness
        I got Jesus   flirtin' with death

ever' day in the coal mines flirtin' with death
        my daddy flirted and my brothers flirted
        and my uncles and cousins
and my daddy got his back broken
        flirtin' with death

brother flirtin' with death   motor cycles, race cars
        not my way   flirtin' with death
sister flirted   I danced around her coffin
high in my hand   same snake caused her death
laid her three weeks baby in her dead arms
sister got holiness   flirtin' with death

I feel holiness   Jesus   I got something
washing feet   laying on hands   dancing the fire dance
        glory glory glory
prayin' for the sign   the wounded blood of Jesus
        on the feet   on the hands   on the head
prayin' three years   for the Jesus sign
        glory hallelujah

in the church house   old snake washed clean
I put him to my shoulders   flirtin' with death
I touch him to my lips   flirtin' with death
flirtin' with death   I raise him to my breast
old velvet lips with his singing tail and lightning breath
I offer velvet lips   my snowy white breast

Jesus Jesus   this old body aint so important
        I got holiness flirtin' with death

Sports Widow

Got anything you want to say
      before the season starts?

Ball one. Ball two. Three games going
      Two tv's and a radio
      My God there are reruns

Boredom. Trouble, you light
      on the sports widow

Bring me a beer
      in his stocking feet
      he stomps his hat upon the floor
Kill the umpire
      O God he is killing me

Rattle pans   slam the door
      step on the dog's tail
How do I like trying to talk
      to a peacock

Sam, I am going to leave you
how would you like to
      kiss a crocodile
You know what I am telling
      you to kiss
He won't move out

I AM SEEING ME

I am seeing me
      through the eyes
      of my cat
I am Cleopatra
      dispensing cream
So beautiful
      as to be gazed on
      forever
The mystery of me
      reflected in your eyes
reflected in the jealousy
      of your eyes
yellow green jealous eyes
Purr your love song
      in the heaven
      of my lap.

LAST PARTY

If I had died younger, I would have
      wanted
My love to hold my hand and forever
      be my love
And kneel on my grave and drown me
      with his tears

Now close the lid as a hymnal is closed
      in church
Just some old women to sit an hour
      and tell
Each other bits of gossip and glance my way
      and say
Young she looks and well and so peaceful

Just a little get-together
And when the gossip lags to glance
      my way
As I was one of them

Just some old women friends
      to come and bide a spell
Just some old women smoothing wrinkles
      from their gowns
As over their specs and under their specs
      my judgment they pronounce
For love has ways of going away
And little children cry too loud
When news and gossip peters out
I would like sitting a last hour with me
Some old women I have known.

II. And Beyond

Refugees

For those who flee the floods and fires
    put a well beside the road
Let there be shade trees
    the bed soft there under
Let hands reach out filled with food
Hold back the rains and mud
Remove the clods that cause the stumbling
Lighten the loads of babies and brothers
Let the nights under the trees or in the ditches
    be undisturbed
    for strength to meet the day
Gentle Savior, look down in pity
On those fleeing the floods and fires.

Noah's Animals

"Shem,
    take with you the fowls you fed the grain.
Ham,
    go with your beasts who provided the milk.
Japheth,
    you fed the winged ones;
    take the winged ones with you."

Old Noah stood barefooted ordering the parade.
He stood barefooted with his galluses hitched high.

On that morning,
    when the rains ceased coming
    through the rotting roof of the ark,
On that morning
    of the great silence,
    preceding the great exodus.
On that morning,
    Ham hit the great pachyderm's toes
    and the pachyderm flapped his ears.
He raised his trunk and saluted old Noah.
    He trumpeted to his mate
    balancing on the far side of the ark
    and together they swung about in line.

The great exodus started.
    Those who came in two by two
    exited by threes, by fives, by sixes,
For there had been, during the great deluge,
    bornings and no dyings.
There was a scramble and a stampede
    each on his own survival course,
    each resuming his original nature,
where the lion, his claws unsheathed,
    no longer lay down by the lamb,
Where the cat took kittens in her mouth,

Where little opossums hung in their mother's pouch.
Noah's wife flapped her apron
    to shoo along the winged things.
Then Mrs. Noah stood still:
    she stood real still,
In that old rotting ark that was waterlogged,
    with a leaking roof
    and all her buckets full of rain water.

A young buffalo calf passed by.
    Mrs. Noah remembered the black bundle
    that was the buffalo calf
    dropped in the early morning
As all the animals gave room
    then circled around,
    inspecting and respecting
    the mystery of new life.

Mrs. Noah washed and eased the buffalo mother,
    her strutted udder caked with milk,
    the lifesaving milk.
The smell of milk buds floated through the air.
Some nursed simultaneously (stealing the milk) with the buffalo calf,
the lion and the lamb lapped milk
    in a gourd and lay down together,
    under a suspension of nature's laws,
    each aiding the other.
Who was nursing off of whom was of no concern.

On that morning
    the sea came alive with its own;
Things began lifting their heads out of the sand;
The black rocks dried off
    and something reptilian lay on the rocks;
A loon looked and found under the sand
    white pebbles to line his gizzard.
Little horns itched and butted the clay banks;
The big sun smoked his pipe

and his smoke lay in the valleys
And wreathed the peaks, irised by the rainbow.
On that morning,
    Old Noah stood with his legs apart
    and snapped his galluses.

He stood barefooted with his britches
    up to his knees and his legs bowed
    like the rainbow is bowed.
He looked toward his animals,
    "I'm giving the Lord the credit."
He looked toward Mrs. Noah
    and his man nature was coming back,
    from under the dispensation,
    for five months is a long while.
"Woman, this quietness is great. By jinks."

Mrs. Noah did not feel delivered
    from any covenant.
"Don't be getting any ideas.
Who is going to clean up this mess?"

She looked at the black hole in the roof,
    where some blue sky was showing,
But this window to heaven did not impress Mrs. Noah.
She was assembling her brooms and mops
    and tightening up her apron strings,
    and heading toward her buckets and tubs,
Full of rainwater from that old leaking roof.
    "This is giving me a headache,"

On that morning
    that great drying out morning, of the great exodus,
When all the animals left Noah and Mrs. Noah
    all alone
    in an empty boat
    with an old rotting roof
    and a mess to clean up.

BOY

*(neither Vietnamese nor American
fathered and left behind by a soldier)*

Papa-san, American man
      I not speak those things
           to anyone
      Why you not come back?
      Why your come back is so long?

      As I drive ducks out to the river
      the cry in my heart is you
      In lantern parade I light
           my light for you

Each day
      I bow before your picture
           many times
      I keep safe in box off your coat
           two buttons

Where you went
      The sampan sail into red moon
           sun
      I look always across water
      from where you come
      Have proud to know
           I can count American now
      I count the strawberry moon
           down
           until he downs in sea

Today I decide
      If you do not come soon
           I will come find you.

SHULAMMITE GIRL

Song of Solomon 6:13, I Kings 1:34

Who were you, little Shulammite girl?
            how did you do
      so rash a deed to Solomon?
          Not that Solomon
   not that one, surely.
He of all the wisdom and glory,
Of all the splendors and harems of gold.

Little country girl, were you like the dawn?
         Bright as the sun,
        as old Sol wrote,
    in that love sick poem,
    pleading you to be his.
You chose love, love with your shepherd boy.
      You had given your word and stuck to it.
      Like a gazelle from a garden of doves,
        You come to us,
        Like the dawn,
Beautiful as the sun,
bright as the moon,
When you told old Sol . . .
        with a resounding *NO* . . .
           . . . to *Cram It*.

INDIAN—ULAGU

No more
will warriors chase the huge wasp
    Ulagu
He who carried off children to mountaintops

A thousand years before Columbus
    the Great Spirit
told Robert White Eagle
    the noble savage at Clinches
Enclose your village with palisades
    circular or ovoid
Bury your infants inside houses
Plant your corn beans squash outside
    watch for Ulagu
from the bald spots
where the Great Spirit cleared the mountain top
rolled oldest of rocks down mountain
    pink feldspar the cranberry gneiss
    shot through with bands of mica
So, the Great Spirit
    created the bare spots
the balds for Navajo to chant
    the world into being
    at daybreak
So did the Great Spirit
    create the balds the bare spots
    for Cherokee
    sentries and lookouts
    to watch for Ulagu
Where the Great Spirit
    cleared the bald spots
    made the bare spots
to keep watch forever
and save the children
    from the huge wasp
    Ulagu!

SOLDIER SOLDIER No. 2

Tell me soldier as we lie here
The medics won't get here in time
Could we talk? There's none to talk to
Through this barbed wire
      mud, blood and grime
Reach and grasp your hand in mine.

Tell me soldier
Is your pain the same as mine?
Tell me of your mother
Tell me of your brother.
Did you pray God for victory
      same as I?

What was it you fought for
Liberty, love, God, country?
I could learn from you
You from me.

Tell me soldier
Tell me of your God.
I will tell of mine
I would not change your ways
Nor you change me from mine.

Had we met upon that field
Honor would have bound us
Now death from a distant clime
Has found us
In new loyalty bound us
Makes us comrades in the end
I wish I could understand.
I cling to a hand extended

The battle is over
No breath of cannons in the air
No bombs burst low or mushrooms high
"To battle stations all."
Flesh moved out flesh
Eternity was there in the barracks.
We were poor boys
Sent to kill poor boys.
Your answer grows a weaker "Ja."

SOLDIER SOLDIER No. 3

Like heroes from an old story
Destined never to be old soldiers
Just young ones to lie down and die.

Ten million heartbeats
Of the strength of youth
    propelling forward
    with no pause.
Their unmatched fortitude
The unmatched mettle
    of young courage.
Brave and furious
Children that went out to battle
and to die.

Blow distant trumpets
For the last good-byes.
Blow for those left to weep
Mary Mother, schoolmates
Young wives, buddies
    comrades in arms

In your brief remembering
Forgo tears at the wall.
What is left to know?
Blow distant trumpets
For the last good-byes
For children who went out to die.
The distant trumpet calls
    to a greater adventure
        Leaving a distant echo, "Ja."

No. 10 BOOM BOOM GIRL

(Vietnamese prostitute with venereal disease)

        Incongruous,
In this stall, waiting for curtains to part,
Under red deceiving light, from its lengthy cord,
To pull the hair over the eyes,
To sway back and forth, one time or two,
And mourn a water buffalo, who ate green
            bamboo shoots

        Strange, as the
Buffalo is dead, that I am alive.
I think it another way; I am dead while it is
The buffalo, who pads, crunches, and
Mulls in his mouth the tender shoots. That
Great severance took the good back, a bird and I used
            to ride on.

        Tiny bells chime,
And the beast will part the curtains, and
Lovers will loose the high fashioned,
High piled hair, that covers the face,
That covers the heart, and stroke and caress
The long black strands, for that is the way
            to begin.

        Latticed bamboo
Made a screen where I watched
The beast burn my hooch house,
And caused to be buried all my relatives.
The buffalo lay all swollen, bloated-rotting,
Stiff legs stretched, upward-pointing,
            to the moon.

> The house was mine.
> I still can see my house, but
> None now can for its black ruin; the bamboo made
> A lattice over the moon; the plum tree flung its
> Snowbank of blossoms as I took to the road and
> Dared not look back because of the nothingness, which is
> > why I left.

> In the city,
> No longer Li but Lilita, I warn my lovers,
> "You have stayed too late. Stay later.
> The beast is out and the street is deserted.
> All know this; you are green not to know. Part
> The curtains, see how deserted the street is, and
> > stay inside."

> The body must
> Have bread; piasters will buy both bread and body.
> When the beast, who already has the body, asks
> For the soul, I will pretend to be not sane and say,
> "I sent it already by the long-tailed blackbird, now
> Sitting on the black bough of
> > the plum tree."

> Because there is
> No relative, no buffalo, no hooch house, the
> Pock-marked road is long for ever getting back.
> Here personalities are numbered, A-1, OK, No. 2
> And I am No. 10. Between the kilos—taxi girl, butterfly,
> Hooch maid, boot polisher—I'll cut your throat, crying,
> > "Crocodile."

> Because I have
> No bamboo lattice to hide me, because tiny
> Bells are wind chimes on my heart, a blackbird
> Who sat upon the buffalo's back flew my soul away,
> And sits with it, beside the moon, on the black bough of the
> Plum tree, miming buffalo shadows, mid
> > bamboo shoots.

NIT OF A LOUSE

I am the coyote
        bringing game
to my mate
        caught in a trap
        in her need to eat.
I am the coyote returning
from soaking my fur
        in water.
My mate licks the water
        from my fur.
I stand by until death
        though I could run free.

LEARNING

Butterfly tattoo on my shoulder.
        Workin' at Roses
Bought myself
        a pair of punk glasses
with polka dots all over
        Nails painted black
riding a red Corvette
        in a short leather skirt.

No good
        I got hind goated.

Followin' that man to Alaska
        sleepin' in the car
        payin' for every hot dog
        peein' in the woods
        along that 15,000 mile highway
No good.
        Did'n' work out.

Learnin' came later
        There was a lot to learn.
        I learned.
        I learned.

Learnin' every day is Judgment Day.
To find hidden treasure
        read the Bible.
Mornin' is a good time to pray.
        Gets the gates of the day open.

Got me a guardian angel
Got me a magic wand
        for scaring away—
so I wouldn't be hind goated.

I'm tellin' you my magic word.
No.
You go seekin' your own.
Wise men are still seekin'.

See me.
    Shootin' down memories
    Crossin' the Rubicon
    Stompin' the blues.
Knowin' knowin' sure.
    The best sex organs
    are ears and brain.

Learnin' not to get hind goated
    Oh I learned.
It came late. But it came each day
    along the way.
Thanks to the butterfly tattoo
    on my shoulder.
Learnin'
    birth from the caterpillar
    death from the cocoon
resurrection from that butterfly.

Learnin' not to get hind goated.
    I learned
    Oh, I learned.

MUTATIONS

These are the barns where old men play
      with rats that have no hair or eyes.

The old men have no hair or eyes
      on little boy bodies with faces like ET
      old, as from a strange and rare disease.

Their masters are the bats.
The old men are playthings of the bats
      in a curious kind of touching,
      with strange sounds, talking in clicks.

The light from a ball of fire
      that left the earth loose from its hinges
      which blinded the old men and rats
      did not blind the bats already
      blind and safe in cave recesses.

Nor did the mushroom cloud
      that caused a collision of stars
      harm the barn or any manmade structure
      but changed old men's brains
      to stand on stems as smooth as mushrooms
      with bats emerging as their kings.

At night the old men melt down into slugs
      that push along on one foot
      and leave trails of slime
      to seed and sprout making new old men
      to last through a day
      playing in the barns with bats
      playing their play briefly
Starting the next billion years all over.

From PLUTO

Not the dog. The planet.
Poor old Pluto
  poking along
  plodding along at 2.9 m/per/sec. . .
No wonder
It takes you 245.4 years
  to orbit the sun....

You Pluto.
They found you
  so far out, so dark, so cold
On the edge of our solar system
A snow bath of icy water
  rock and methane gas.
Close enough to get whispers
  from alien worlds.

From LOST IN SPACE

Who will find this pile of stones
Who will find this pile of bones
They tell no tale of heat or cold . . .
Be this my final resting place
This tale is told of loneliness.

Poor drawings scratched stone on stone
No monolith but a hundred stones
Hundreds piled onto this mound
My monument to loneliness.

In this place there is no time
Numbers and hours do not apply
As memory goes and I levitate
into some ethereal medium space

I look back to see bleached bones
My bequest to the stars . . .
Only this eternity of no beginning
With no end to loneliness
Is real.

From RIDING IN SPACE

I have seen the village farms
  creeping up the sides of Mt. Vesuvius
and witnessed the parking light
  of the aurora
  in its electric magnetic storm.
In space I have
  witnessed ocean chasms
  pulling apart
and seen the wakes of ships
  spreading hundreds of miles.

Out of the swirling speed
  of clouds and storms
  into the heart of a hurricane,
I fly over vast meteor craters,
  over icebergs half the size of Rhode Island
  floating out from Antarctica
over crust heaving into vast folds,
  tectonic folds crashing together
  on land or under sea.

I see Lake Baikal
  three miles deep
  with 400 rivers feeding,
  pushed out where continents still collide.

From . . . OF CIRCLES

Men in saloons in their beer
    talking in circles
fresh from arctic rigors
fresh from the top of the world
    talking in circles.

Indians and senior citizens
    hopping around in circle dances.
George laughing
    at his cow flops and horse apples.
The common chicken
    turning circles in the dust.
Circles of raindrops
    on the face of the pond.
Old John lost in his circle
    trying to find his way home.

The family circle
    of a mother's arms
    around the child.
Circles of eternity
    in God's encircling arms.

Planets to asteroids
    to particles of dust.
Words like forever—
    forever, ethereal, perfection
connecting no end no beginning
    our circular destiny.

Meg, Beth, John
    finding circles
    for their fingers.

Notes

page 16

From an old rhyme, Pulling Off the Petals

page 18.

Change in pronouns at the end due to an old superstition. Do not speak directly ill about the dead.

page 44

"Crocodile" was Vietnamese street slang for "I'll kill you."

page 45

"Nit of a Louse" is a term for something almost as small as the egg of a louse or parasite. I use the term to refer to small poems, such as this one and "Mosquito on Nose" on page 20.

About the Author

LOU CRABTREE, born in 1913, has lived most of her life in Washington County, Virginia. During her active life she has taught school, farmed, directed the Rock of Ages band, conducted regional auditions for the American Academy of Dramatic Arts, co-directed a bicentennial play, and lectured on many subjects. Her first book, a collection of short stories entitled *Sweet Hollow*, was published by LSU Press in 1983, in her 70th year, and is now in its fourth printing.

She has won many honors for her writing, including a PEN/Faulkner award, and poetry awards from *Laurel Review* and *Shenandoah*, and from the Poetry Society of Virginia. In 1988 she was declared a "Laureate in Literature" by the Commonwealth of Virginia, and a one-woman show based on her stories and poems was presented by Cleo Partington at Barter Theatre, and later toured throughout the region.

The widow of Homer Crabtree, and the mother of five children, she lives in Abingdon, Virginia.